EMBRACING
REALITY

A Directive for Achieving Sustainability
in the Twenty-First Century

JEB TAYLOR

Embracing Reality: A Directive for Achieving Sustainability in the Twenty-First Century

Jeb Taylor

Print ISBN: 978-1-54390-654-7

eBook ISBN: 978-1-54390-655-4

11-2017

To future generations, whose quality of life will depend upon the wisdom of the decisions that we make today.

CONTENTS

INTRODUCTION   1

PART I: CHANGING PERSPECTIVES   3

    1: Progressive Social Behavior   3

    2: Sustainability   4

    3: Raising Awareness   4

    4: Resistance to Raising Public Awareness   8

    5: Interdependency and Cooperation   9

    6: Accepting Responsibility   10

PART II: TRANSCENDING FAITH   11

    7: Religious SIGs   11

       Judaism   13

       Christianity   17

       Islam   26

    8: Political SIGs   34

    9: Economic SIGs   35

PART III: RAISING AWARENESS   37

    10: Sources of Information   37

       Parents   37

       Schools   38

       Places of Worship   39

       The Media   39

       Social Media   41

PART IV: EMBRACING REASON   43

    11: Religion   43

    12: Government   43

       Religious Influences   44

Political Influences   45

Economic Influences   46

Establishing Rational Government   47

13: Commerce   47

PART V: ACHIEVING SUSTAINABILITY   49

14: Reprieval   49

15: Population   50

State Security   50

Perpetuation of Religions   51

"Right" to Procreate   52

Population Reduction   52

16: Pollution   54

Carbon Dioxide   54

Climate Change   55

Ocean Acidification   57

Curbing Carbon Dioxide Pollution   59

Electrical Generation   59

Alternative Energy Sources   60

Nuclear Energy   60

Transportation   63

Diet   63

17: Conservation   66

Terrestrial Flora   66

Terrestrial Fauna   68

Marine Fauna   69

Progressive Behavior   71

EPILOGUE   73

INTRODUCTION

In personal correspondence with renowned Canadian environmentalist Farley Mowat regarding the future prospects of humankind, he stated:

Homo sapiens is a lost cause . . . the sooner we become extinct, the better the prospects are for the ongoing survival and evolution of animate creation.

Farley devoted much of his life to raising public awareness and encouraging sustainable behavior—so the fact that he gave up on us as a species should be regarded as an alarming indication that we are not only severely deluded and wantonly exploitive, but that we maintain a perverse determination to remain so.

Our exploitive behavior is severely diminishing Earth's biota and resources—to the degree that if we do not raise our awareness and adopt sustainable behavior in the very near future, we will exhaust Earth's capacity to support us, and civilization will collapse.

If self-induced collapse is to be our destiny, then Farley was right—the sooner it happens, the better it will be for the rest of animate creation.

But collapse does not have to be our destiny—at least not in the foreseeable future—at least not due to overexploitation. We can achieve sustainability if we raise our awareness and learn to rely exclusively on reason to guide our behavior.

This sounds pretty straightforward, but raising our awareness will be difficult because religious, political, business, and other ideological special interest groups (SIGs) coerce us—through expansive indoctrination campaigns—to rely on them and their irrational dogmas to guide our behavior.

The following discussion is dedicated to establishing global sustainability in the twenty-first century. Sustainability must be global because individual nations are too interdependent to establish sustainability on their own—and it must be established in the twenty-first century because escalating resource depletion will make it impossible to achieve after then.

Establishing sustainability can only be accomplished by raising *global* awareness—which will require the exclusive reliance on reason to guide our behavior—which will require the transcendence of faith in ideological SIGs and their dogmas.

Adherents will undoubtedly find this difficult, but transcending faith and embracing reason is incredibly liberating. The universe is a rational place, so when reality is embraced, everything begins to make sense.

Besides, because embracing reality is requisite to establishing sustainability—it is the only acceptable option available to us.

PART I: CHANGING PERSPECTIVES

It is easy to dodge our responsibilities, but we cannot dodge the consequences of dodging our responsibilities.

—Josiah Charles Stamp

1: Progressive Social Behavior

When our ancestors adopted agriculture twelve thousand years ago, they inadvertently crossed a threshold between primitive and civilized existences. This crossing committed all future generations to an increasing reliance on progressive technology—*and* the need to adopt progressive, sustainable social behavior commensurate with the developing technologies.

We have learned to incorporate progressive technology into our material cultures incredibly well, but we have failed to adopt the progressive, sustainable social behavior commensurate with these developing technologies into our social cultures.

In other words, we are technologically progressive—but socially conservative.

This is an untenable situation because nearly every problem that threatens civilization today, from suicide bombings and wars to pollution and overpopulation, can be traced directly or indirectly back to the disparity that exists between progressive technological development and conservative social behavior.

We either have to *regress* technologically—or *progress* socially—to achieve sustainability.

Trying to do both is leading to chronic overconsumption of natural resources, the extermination of many thousands of plant and animal species, and irreparable damage to the environment.

Developing technologies have enabled us to forestall the consequences of these transgressions by employing increasingly efficient methods of harvesting *dwindling* resources. However, even the most efficient methods will not enable us to harvest resources once they are completely *depleted*.

Regressing technologically is not a viable option, so it is imperative that we progress socially.

2: Sustainability

Before discussing how to establish sustainability, it is important to understand what it is, and what it is not. First of all, it is important to realize that sustainability is not a static state. Earth is a dynamic planet affected by shifting tectonic plates, volcanic eruptions, orbital perturbations, variances in solar radiation, meteoric impacts from space, and so on. All of which profoundly affect Earth's climate—which profoundly affects Earth's capacity to sustain biota, including us.

When climatic conditions are favorable, Earth might be able to sustain as many as 3 billion people, but during times of unfavorable climatic conditions, it might be fewer than 1 billion.

Consequently, it is essential to realize that sustainability is dynamic.

3: Raising Awareness

Raising awareness is requisite to establishing progressive social behavior. Unfortunately, *repressing* awareness is so prevalent in our cultures today that no provisions have been made to even discuss the subject objectively.

It is essential that we do so now, so the definitions of the following words have necessarily been refined slightly to make this possible.

Terms Associated With Reason:

rational information: information based on reason or logic,

knowledge: conclusions based on rational information—*amendable,*

education: the conveyance of rational information and knowledge—intending to inform—*dynamic,*

awareness: a positive state of consciousness resulting from the accumulation of rational information and knowledge through education, and

reality: the universe as perceived from a rational perspective.

Rational information, knowledge, education, awareness, and reality are linked together because they are related to reason.

Terms Associated With Faith:

irrational information: information conceived through imagination, or, if religious in nature, allegedly through divination;

dogmas: conclusions based on irrational information—*incontrovertible;*

indoctrination: the conveyance of irrational information and dogmas—intending to influence—*static;*

delusion: a negative state of consciousness resulting from the assimilation of irrational information and dogmas through indoctrination; and

fantasy: the universe as perceived from an irrational perspective.

Irrational information, dogmas, indoctrination, delusion, and fantasy are linked together because they are related to faith.

We are all born ignorant. During our lives, we accumulate rational information and knowledge through education, which raises our awareness; but we also assimilate irrational information and dogma through indoctrination, which deludes us.

It has been said that the greatest impediment to progress is ignorance, but that is not true. Ignorance is a void that can be filled with knowledge. The greatest impediment to progress is delusion.

Surveys indicate that 85 percent of the world's population believes in one god or another, which means that 85 percent of the world's population has been indoctrinated to maintain faith in religious SIGs and their dogmas. This fact means that at least 85 percent of the world's population is moderately to severely deluded.

It is the 15 percent of the population that has resisted or transcended religious indoctrination that concerns us now, because there is a strong possibility that they are *rationalists.*

Rationalists do not believe *in* gods for the same reason that they do not believe *in* anything—they regard all beliefs as irrational. When there is reason to support the existence of something, its existence is known. Therefore, it does not have to be believed.

When it comes to assessing the merits of rational perspectives, it is pertinent to note that it has been rationalists, utilizing rational information and knowledge, who have enabled civilization to progress as far as it has. And by logical extension, it will be rationalists, utilizing rational information and knowledge, who will help raise public awareness enough to establish sustainability.

Conversely, it is irrationalists, utilizing irrational information and dogmas, who are keeping us from raising our awareness and establishing sustainable behavior.

Consequently, we need to do everything we can to encourage the conveyance of rational information and knowledge through education—and to discourage the preservation of dogmas and the conveyance of irrational information through indoctrination.

The best way to accomplish this is by learning to evaluate information objectively from two different perspectives:

- What are the motives for its dissemination?
- What is the plausibility of its content?

There are two primary motives for disseminating information:

- to *inform* (through education) and
- to *influence* (through indoctrination).

While neither motive is necessarily accurate or inaccurate, information that is intended to inform is far more likely to be rational than information that is intended to influence. Information offered by a scientist regarding the environmental effects of burning coal, for example, is far more likely to be rational than information offered by a spokesperson for the coal industry. In the same way, information contained in a book on biology regarding the origins of life is more likely to be rational than information contained in the Torah or Old Testament.

When it comes to assessing the plausibility of information, it is worth considering some sage advice attributed to Buddha:

> *Believe nothing, no matter where you read it, or who said it, no matter if I have said it, unless it agrees with your own reason and your own common sense.*

We tend to think of common sense as intuitive, but that is not the case. Common sense is actually developed through objective experience (nurture not nature). Unfortunately, individuals who have been indoctrinated with irrational information and dogmas—which is most of us—have proportionately diminished capacities to exercise common sense.

Rational and irrational perspectives are mutually exclusive. The more we believe, the less we can know—and the more we know, the less we will believe. Consequently, it is critically important that we transcend our irrational beliefs so that we can accumulate more knowledge.

4: Resistance to Raising Public Awareness

Unfortunately, there is tremendous resistance to raising public awareness. Rationalists are generally free to utilize reason in artificial development. However, powerful religious, political, and economic SIGs generally prohibit rationalists from becoming directly involved in social development because they rely on deluded publics to support them and their dogmas.

In the past, when rationalists attempted social *pro*activity, they were ostracized, imprisoned, or executed for dissidence. In light of this oppressive treatment, rationalists have understandably become extremely *re*active.

Current events now mandate that they become more proactive. Only rationalists can help adherents through the oppressive maze created by ideological SIGs that retards awareness.

Unfortunately, appealing to adherents' common sense will not be enough to persuade them to transcend faith, because their perspectives have been severely compromised through indoctrination.

In order to accomplish that goal, rationalists will have to convince dogmatic adherents that (1) civilization can collapse; that (2) collapse is imminent; that (3) collapse will be permanent; and (4) that their children and grandchildren will be subjected to unimaginable hardships when it does collapse.

And above all else, adherents must be educated to the fact that their ideological SIGs are not divine, and that their dogmas are not incontrovertible.

We must realize that maintaining the status quo is a death sentence for civilization. We can maintain faith in ideological SIGs and their dogmas—or we can transcend them and learn to rely exclusively on reason to guide our behavior. However, we cannot do both.

Before deciding which option is best, it is worth considering that civilization can survive indefinitely without faith, but it cannot survive a day without reason.

5: Interdependency and Cooperation

The adoption of progressive social behavior that our ancestors inadvertently committed us to when they crossed the threshold between primitive and civilized existences, includes the establishment of *global* interdependency and cooperation.

This has understandably been a challenge for us. For the vast majority of our species' history, interdependency and cooperation rarely reached beyond extended family members within tribes. Most other tribes were regarded as competitors or enemies.

After the adoption of agriculture, however, social groups quickly expanded to encompass multi-family villages—then multi-village states—then multi-state nations—and eventually, multi-nation coalitions.

It is generally not recognized as such, but the transition from intratribal interdependency and cooperation to international interdependency and cooperation is one of our species' greatest accomplishments.

We have progressed a long way in this regard, but establishing sustainability will require the integration of comprehensive global interdependency and cooperation. Unfortunately, many ideological SIGs promote extremely polarizing dogmas that encourage national independence, competition, and exploitation.

These are not perspectives that lead to sustainability. In fact, *every* nation in the past that relied on independence, competition, and exploitation to advance or maintain itself eventually collapsed.

It is essential that we now transcend our conservative perspectives regarding independency and competition and adopt progressive perspectives encompassing comprehensive, global interdependency, and cooperation. These are requisite conditions to achieving sustainability.

6: Accepting Responsibility

Almost everyone recognizes that civilization is in trouble, but we all seem resigned to relying on people in positions of authority to save it. This is a huge mistake. Today's leaders are generally individuals who have been thoroughly indoctrinated with religious, political, and economic dogmas and feel compelled to defend and advance them.

This means that today's leaders are chronically deluded and incapable of directing progressive social behavior.

Like it or not, the responsibility for saving civilization lies with us, and requires that we raise our awareness and adopt progressive social behavior. But before we can do that, we will have to transcend our faith in religious, political, and economic SIGs and their dogmas.

PART II: TRANSCENDING FAITH

Religion is regarded by the common people as true, by the wise as false, and by the rulers as useful.

—Seneca (Roman philosopher, first-century CE)

7: Religious SIGs

The following chapter addresses religious SIGs and their dogmas far more objectively than is customary. The reason for this is that they are frequently promoted as divine and inviolate, which makes them, once accepted, extremely difficult to transcend. Many of the problems that threaten civilization stem from religious SIGs.

A premise of this discussion is that maintaining faith in religious SIGs and dogmas precludes the raising of awareness—a requisite condition for establishing sustainability. Consequently, challenging the divine and inviolate status of religious SIGs and their dogmas is critical to this premise.

It is unlikely that adherents will consider transcending faith in their religious SIGs and their dogmas unless they are shown—beyond a shadow of doubt—that they are neither divine nor inviolate.

• • •

According to the Religious Tolerance website, there are nineteen major religions, divided into 270 large religious groups. These religious groups are further divided into more than 30,000 smaller religious SIGs competing for recognition and public support.[1]

In this discussion, we will specifically address the Abrahamic religions: Judaism, Christianity, and Islam because Christianity and Islam are the two largest and most influential religions, and all three of them are at the forefront of much of the polarity and conflict that exists in the world today.

The Abrahamic religions are based on laws and directives recorded in scriptures. Each religion claims that its scripture was provided to them by God through *their* prophets—and each maintains that *its* scripture is the *true* scripture, and that only those who adhere to it are following God's laws and serving his will.

If any religion is in possession of scripture provided to them by God, then it could arguably be regarded as divine—but none is. The best that religions can claim is that they are in possession of accurate facsimiles of scriptures provided to them by God—which, of course, they all do.

It is not possible to prove or disprove scriptural divinity. However, we can determine whether scriptures are rational or irrational, and thus draw some conclusions regarding the likelihood of them being divine or mortal.

God is regarded as omniscient by Jews, Christians, and Muslims, so it is reasonable to assume that scriptures provided by God would be completely rational. This does not mean that rational scriptures are necessarily divine—only that divine scriptures would necessarily have to be rational.

By logical extension, we can also assume that an omniscient God would not provide irrational scriptures—so those that are irrational cannot be not divine.

In other words, irrational scriptures are mortal, and need not be regarded as inviolate.

---

1   http://www.religioustolerance.org/worldrel.htm

Judaism

- The Jewish scripture is the Tanakh. It contains:
- The Torah (Pentateuch, or the Five Books of Moses)
- The Nevi'im (Prophets)
- The Ketuvim (Writings)

Jews believe that the Torah was given to them by God through their prophet Moses in the 1300s BCE. The oldest known Torah is in a copy of the Tanakh known as the Leningrad Codex, which was written in 1009 CE. Consequently, 2,300 years separate the alleged original writing of the Torah by Moses and the earliest known extant copy of it.

Jews claim that today's Torah is an accurate facsimile of the text allegedly written by Moses more than three thousand years ago. Whether that claim is true or is not is irrelevant to this discussion. Our concern is determining whether the Torah is divine or mortal—rational or irrational.

With that in mind, we will examine the biblical account of Noah and the flood.

Genesis 6:9

God began to recognize the wickedness of humankind and decided to:

> … *blot out from the earth the men whom I created—men together with beasts, creeping things, and birds of the sky for I regret that I made them.*

God directed Noah to build an ark to hold: his family, male and female members of every species on Earth, and enough provisions to support them for an extended period of time.

When the ark was completed and everyone and everything was loaded into it, God made it rain for forty days and forty nights—until the waters covered the tallest mountains. The ark remained adrift for eight months, at which time the water receded, and Noah's family and all of the animals disembarked to repopulate Earth.

There are many irrationalities in Genesis 6:9. The most notable of these are the flood, the ark itself, and the space within the ark.

The Flood

Scientists maintain that throughout most of Earth's history, there has always been about the same amount of water. Water is involved in a continuous cycle from accumulation—to evaporation—to condensation—to precipitation—and then back again to accumulation. This process is known as the hydrologic cycle, and it is essentially a closed cycle.

Heavy local rainfall can cause local flooding, but it cannot raise ocean levels, because evaporated ocean water is the primary source of the condensed water vapor that falls as rain.

Nevertheless, Genesis 7:20-23 states that the deluge covered the tops of all the mountains, killing every animal on Earth. Assuming that God could, and did, preempt the hydrologic cycle—and estimating that the average height above sea level, globally, is around three thousand feet—it would take about 500 million cubic miles of water to cover the tallest mountains.

The heaviest rainfall ever recorded in a single day occurred on an island in the Indian Ocean where it rained *six feet* on January 7, 1966.[2] That was an incredibly heavy rainfall, but nothing compared to the alleged rainfall described in Genesis 7:20-23. In order for rainfall to inundate all of Earth's mountains, it would have to have rained *650 feet*—every day—everywhere on Earth—for forty days.

Another issue to consider is that if the entire Earth had been covered with water, the oceans' salt water and land's fresh waters would have mixed—rendering all water on Earth too salty to support freshwater organisms, and not salty enough to support marine organisms. Additionally, when the water evaporated,[3] it would have deposited enough salt on Earth's surface to render its soil too salty for most terrestrial plants.

---

2   http://www.accuweather.com/en/weather-news/the-greatest-24hour-deluge-in/52828

3   The biblical flood could not recede, because there was no place for the water to recede to.

And perhaps most importantly, there is *no* scientific evidence that such a flood ever occurred.

The Ark

According to Genesis 6:11, God instructed Noah to make the ark 300 cubits long (450 feet) by 50 cubits wide (75 feet) by 30 cubits high (45 feet), with a bottom and two decks.

A full-sized model of the ark was recently built in Kentucky. It required approximately 3.3 million board feet of lumber to complete—or enough lumber[4] to build about 825 single-family homes.[5]

That is an enormous amount of lumber to process, even with modern power tools, which Noah obviously did not have. In fact, he did not even have iron tools. In the twenty-first century BCE when the ark was allegedly built, the only tools that would have been available to Noah would have been primitive stone and bronze hand tools.

It is pertinent to note that a boat built to these specifications would not only be the largest wooden boat ever built, it would be the largest wooden structure ever built. Consequently, it is reasonable to assume that Noah did not build it.

Proponents claim that the ark would have been extremely seaworthy. However, before steel ships were built, builders of wooden ships experimented with a number of large hull designs and determined that the practical maximum length for wooden ships, even ones built with modern tools and technologies, was less than 200 feet. Wooden ships longer than that were built and tested, but all of them failed to perform adequately. Even in moderate seas, they flexed too much to remain watertight and required constant pumping to stay afloat.

---

4   https://en.wikipedia.org/wiki/Ark_Encounter

5   http://www.idahoforests.org/woodhous.htm

Consequently, even if Noah had managed to build the ark, it would not have been seaworthy enough to survive for forty days in a stormy sea.

Space

In Genesis 6:20 God commanded Noah to load two of each animal species[6] into the ark. A great deal of dissension exists regarding how many species were loaded into the ark, but since there are 23,792 *known living* animal species, it is safe to assume that at least one pair of each of these species would have been in the ark in order for them to have survived the flood.

Assuming that each deck of the ark contained 25,000 square feet (the maximum possible), each *pair* of animals would have to have shared a space less than two square feet.[7] This might have been enough for small rodents, but certainly not for the larger animals.

In Genesis 6:22, God commanded Noah to "take of everything that is eaten, and store it away, to serve as food for you and for them."

Accurately determining how much food would have been needed to sustain all the animals on the ark is impossible. However, the Toronto Zoo[8] reports that their 5,816 animals require approximately 1.4 tons of food each day. If that number is multiplied by 4.1 (to reflect the number of animals on the ark), they would have required about 5.7 tons of food each day—or 171 tons each month—or 1,368 tons for eight months.

Estimating how much space that much food would have taken up is also difficult to calculate, but one ton of compressed hay occupies about 128 cubic feet, so 1,368 tons of hay would have occupied approximately 175,104 cubic feet of space—or one entire deck of the ark stacked seven feet high.

---

6   how animal species from areas separated from the Middle East by oceans got there was never addressed

7   if extinct animal species are factored in, then the space would obviously have been much less

8   http://www.torontozoo.com/EducationAndCamps/Elementary/ InformationBooklets/Toronto%20Zoo-%20Facts%20and%20Figures.pdf

Clearly some foods are denser than baled hay, but most forage foods would have been far less dense. In any event, these figures are only intended to give some idea of how implausible it would have been to provide enough food for all the animals in the ark for eight months.

If God was the source of the biblical flood account, it should be completely rational. But it is not. Instead, it is highly irrational.

When Jewish scriptures are evaluated objectively, it becomes clear that many of the accounts are equally irrational. Consequently, it is reasonable to assume that the Tanakh is not divine, which means that Jewish dogmas are not inviolate and that they can be transcended without fear.

Christianity

Judaism is a demanding religion. It requires great devotion and adherence to rituals, including exacting animal sacrifices and offerings. It is also a very exclusive religion, intended to minister specifically to Jews (the descendants of Abraham). Consequently, it has never been tempting for Gentiles to embrace Judaism. These conditions are reflected in its low membership. Even though Judaism is one of the oldest religions, only 0.22 percent of the world's population embraces it.

Although Judaism has never been particularly expansive, Jews tend to be extremely successful—a trait that Gentiles have both resented and envied. One manifestation of envy has been to incorporate aspects of Judaism into their own religions, which brings us to the second of the Abrahamic religions—Christianity.

The Christian scripture is the Holy Bible. It is composed of:

- The Old Testament (which is essentially the Jewish Tanakh), and
- The New Testament.

Many people believe that Christianity was established by Jesus, but that is not true. Jesus co-led a messianic *Jewish* movement started by John the Baptist that encouraged a reaffirmation of *Jewish* faith through baptism.

Christianity was actually established after Jesus was executed in the first century CE by a Roman Jew named Paul—who never met Jesus.

The Holy Bible is composed of two parts: the Old Testament and New Testament. Another aspect of Christianity that many Christians are not aware of is that the Old Testament is the Jewish Tanakh. It was reordered and modified slightly to serve Christian premises better, but it is essentially the same book. Its inclusion in the Holy Bible is puzzling, and may represent the most egregious act of plagiarism ever committed.

In any event, like Jews, Christians believe that the Old Testament contains the actual laws of God—as provided by God to Moses and other Hebrew prophets. However, Christians believe they have been absolved from adherence to those laws through antinomianism, a concept Paul explained in the New Testament (Romans 3:20, 3:28, etc.).

Consequently, it is the New Testament that defines Christianity, and it has a very convoluted history. The oldest known version of the New Testament is in a copy of the Holy Bible known as the Codex Vaticanus, which was written in Greek sometime in the fourth century CE.

Actually, there never was an original New Testament. Different versions of it evolved independently over relatively long periods of time in different areas. Nevertheless, the supporters of each version maintain that *their* version is the only *true* version.

Regardless of the version, the New Testament is quite literally a testament to the birth, life, teachings, death, and resurrection of Jesus. Remarkably, for someone who is so important today, virtually nothing was written about Jesus during his lifetime.

The New Testament is composed of twenty-seven books, including:

- Gospels (outlining Jesus's life)
- Acts (a narrative of the apostles' ministries)
- Twenty-one epistles (letters written to different churches in the Roman Empire)

- Revelation (an apocalyptic prophecy)

These books have been attributed to a number of different authors, but many objective religious historians warn that no one actually knows who wrote much of the New Testament.

What Christians accept regarding Jesus's life comes primarily from the four canonical Gospels: Matthew, Mark, Luke, and John. These Gospels were written thirty to eighty years after Jesus died by unknown authors who probably never met Jesus, witnessed his activities, or listened to his sermons.

The primary purpose of the canonical Gospels was to demonstrate that Jesus was the Jewish Messiah, and to promote his divinity. This was "accomplished" in the Gospels by citing Jesus's lineage back to King David and by citing events in his life that seemed to fulfill Old Testament (Jewish) prophecies. It is pertinent to note, however, that although Christians believe that Jesus was the rightful king of the Jews, Jews do not recognize Jesus as their messiah.

There were many other Christian Gospels available for canonical consideration, but they were rejected. In 185 CE, Irenaeus (bishop of Lyons) selected Matthew, Mark, Luke, and John as *the* canonical Gospels. In *Adversus Haereses*,[9] he explained why. These passages are difficult to read, but they are very important because they established which gospels would be the Canonical Gospels, and the Canonical Gospels form the backbone of the Holy Bible and Christianity.

> *Matthew: Now the Gospels, in which Christ is enthroned, are like these. . . . Matthew proclaims his human birth, saying, "The book of the generation of Jesus Christ, son of David, son of Abraham," and, "The birth of Jesus Christ was in this manner" . . . for this Gospel is manlike, and so through the whole Gospel [Christ] appears as a man of a humble mind, and gentle.*

---

9   http://www.ntcanon.org/Irenaeus.shtml#4_Gospels

Mark: Now the Gospels, in which Christ is enthroned, are like these. . . . But Mark takes his beginning from the prophetic Spirit who comes on men from on high saying, "The beginning of the gospel of Jesus Christ, as it is written in Isaiah the prophet," showing a winged image of the gospel. Therefore he made his message compendious and summary, for such is the prophetic character.

Luke: Now the Gospels, in which Christ is enthroned, are like these. . . . That according to Luke, as having a priestly character, began with the priest Zacharias offering incense to God. For the fatted calf was already being prepared, which was to be sacrificed for the finding of the younger son.

John: Now the Gospels, in which Christ is enthroned, are like these. . . . For that according to John expounds his princely and mighty and glorious birth from the Father, saying, "In the beginning was the Word, and the Word was with God, and the Word was God," and, "All things were made by him, and without him was not any thing made that was made." Therefore, this Gospel is deserving of all confidence, for such indeed is his person.

The Gospels could not possibly be either more or less in number than they are. Since there are four zones of the world in which we live, and four principal winds, while the Church is spread over all the earth, and the pillar and foundation of the Church is the gospel, and the Spirit of life, it fittingly has four pillars, everywhere breathing out incorruption and revivifying men. From this it is clear that the Word, the artificer of all things, being manifested to men gave us the gospel, fourfold in form but held together by one Spirit. As David said, when asking for his coming, "O sitter upon the cherubim, show yourself." For the cherubim have four faces, and their faces are images of the activity of the Son of God. For the first living creature, it says, was like a lion, signifying his active and princely and royal character; the second was like an ox, showing his sacrificial and priestly order;

the third had the face of a man, indicating very clearly his com-
ing in human guise; and the fourth was like a flying eagle, mak-
ing plain the giving of the Spirit who broods over the Church.
Now the Gospels, in which Christ is enthroned, are like these.

Irenaeus claimed that he was able to determine that these particular Gospels were the *correct* Gospels, because he recognized their "God-breathed," or "spirit-breathed," contents. Christian clerics maintain that scripture is inspired by God, and that they can recognize its divinity. They cite 2 Timothy 3:16 in defense of this claim:

All scripture is given by inspiration of God, and is profit-
able for doctrine, for reproof, for correction, for instruction
in righteousness.

Like many religious claims, this one is highly irrational, but it is impossible to disprove.

Truth

Before proceeding further, it is important to explain that the Abrahamic religious concept of *truth* is different from the social definition that we are accustomed to.

Because all Abrahamic religions believe their doctrines are essentially divine, they also believe they represent immutable truths. The ramifications of these interpretations are significant, because their doctrines also maintain that the successful dissemination of their versions of the truth—no matter how it is achieved—is righteous. That attitude has led to the perpetration of a great many unjust acts. They occur in all religions, but more so among the many Christian denominations. In any event, it is important to realize that Abrahamic religious dogmas do not have to be *true* in order for them to be regarded as truths.

The Five Christian Tenets

The Gospels of Matthew, Mark, Luke, and John were allegedly chosen for their "spirit-breathed" content, but they also most closely supported the orthodox beliefs of Irenaeus and other second-century church clerics. Orthodox Christianity rests on five indisputable tenets, that Jesus:

- was born of a virgin,
- was the rightful king of Judea,[10]
- died for our sins,
- was resurrected and ascended into heaven, and
- will return one day to rule Earth.

And one fundamental assumption, that:

- Paul received guidance from Jesus after Jesus's death.

Any Gospel, book, or letter, regardless of its source, that supports these premises is regarded by Christians as *true*, and any that contests them is regarded as *false* or *heretical*.

Paul The "Disciple"

Paul was a Pharisee Jew with Roman citizenship, who, as an adult, converted to the aristocratic Sadducees. Initially, Paul vehemently opposed the messianic Jewish movement that Jesus led. However, when traveling to Damascus several years after Jesus died, Paul allegedly fell from his horse and had a vision where Jesus commissioned him to become a minister (Acts 26:13-14).

At that time, Paul joined the messianic Jewish movement Jesus had led when he was alive, and began to minister to Roman and Greek Gentiles. Jesus's apostles apparently supported Paul's ministry to the Gentiles—but not what he taught. His messages, although captivating, did not conform to

---

10   That Jesus is the rightful king of Judea, according to orthodox Christians, is demonstrated by his alleged fulfillment of Old Testament prophecies.

the messianic Jewish movement they subscribed to. Listed in the following are uniquely Christian concepts that Paul initiated:

- Jesus died for humankind's sins (1 Corinthians 15:3).
- Jesus was buried and rose again on the third day (1 Corinthians 15:4).
- Jesus ascended to heaven (Romans 8:34).
- Jesus will return to rule over the Earth (1 Thessalonians 4:13-18).

Paul also taught the following:

- Those who accept the atonement of Jesus's sacrifice would be given eternal life (1 Corinthians 15:51-54 and 1 Thessalonians 4:13-18).
- The Lord's Supper, or Eucharist, identifies wine as Christ's blood, bread as Christ's flesh, etc. (1 Corinthians 3:16-17 and 11:23-28).

And most disturbing to Jesus's apostles, Paul claimed that the Laws of Moses did not have to be observed if adherents accepted Jesus as their savior (Galatians 3:24-25).

There can be little doubt that Paul devoutly believed in his mission, and he was almost solely responsible for creating Christian premises 3, 4, and 5, that Jesus:

- died for humankind's sins,
- was resurrected and ascended into heaven, and
- will return one day to rule the Earth.

Although Paul established Christianity, using Jesus as its figurehead, Christians need to realize that Jesus, his apostles, and his disciples were devout Jews—not Christians. Consequently, Paul did not promote the teachings of Jesus; *he promoted the teachings of Jesus according to Paul.* Regardless of how improbable Paul's claims were regarding his commissionship with Jesus, *Christianity is based upon them.*

Dissension

Since the inception of Christianity, there has been a great deal of dissension regarding the relationship between God, Jesus, and the Holy Spirit. In 325 CE, in an attempt to address those issues, Emperor Constantine headed a council at Nicea attended by three hundred bishops, priests, and deacons.

The council proclaimed that God (the Father), Jesus (the Son), and the Holy Spirit were actually one godhead. This arrangement is known as the Trinity, and it enabled Jesus to be divine and still be eligible for Judean kingship.[11]

Establishing the Trinity was intended to unify Christendom, which in some ways it did. However, disagreements regarding whether the Holy Spirit came from the Father and the Son, or just the Father, polarized Christians into two separate groups that eventually led to the division of Christendom into Eastern (Greek Orthodox) and Western (Roman Catholic) groups in 1054 CE.

The Biblical Jesus

Many Christians are not aware of it, but the biblical Jesus shared many similarities to earlier mythological man-gods, such as Mithra, Osiris, Krishna, Dionysus, Buddha, and so on—all of whom allegedly possessed more than two of the following traits:

- born of a virgin,
- born on December 25,
- birth was attended by wise men/angels,
- performed miracles,
- died for the salvation of humankind,
- resurrected on or around the spring equinox,
- ascended into heaven/nirvana, and
- promised to return one day to rule the Earth.

---

11   http://www.mgr.org/ConstantinePart1.html

An innovative disputation of these pagan precedents was offered by the second-century Christian apologist, Justin Martyr. When confronting their similarities, he claimed that the devil was able to anticipate not only the coming of Jesus, but also the conditions surrounding his birth, life, death, and resurrection—and imitate them thousands of years before they actually occurred.

Martyr did not question the historicity of these other man-gods—only their originality. It is also pertinent to note that Jesus's divinity was being questioned to the degree that Martyr felt compelled to defend it even *before* the New Testament was canonized.

The Historical Jesus

Since the biblical Jesus wasn't the only, or even the first, man-god to allegedly possess these "divine" traits, should he also be regarded as a mythical man-god? Absolutely! There is no evidence that the biblical Jesus ever existed. However, most religious historians do believe that a Galilean Jew named Jesus did exist, and that he:

- was born between 7 and 2 BCE in Nazareth,
- preached a messianic form of Judaism to small groups of mostly disenfranchised Jews,
- may have believed he was the rightful king of the Jews,
- overturned the tables of the money changers in Herod's Temple during Passover, and
- was arrested for sedition and crucified by the Romans sometime between 27 and 36 CE.

None of Jesus's sermons were recorded during his lifetime, so we do not actually know what Jesus's messages were. All of the quotes attributed to him in the New Testament were contrived by others—most of whom probably never heard Jesus's sermons. The quotes have been given legitimacy by church clerics who claimed to recognize their "spirit-breathed" contents, but they reflect Christian rather than Jewish values, so their claims, although well intended, are spurious.

Even though Jesus's sermons were never recorded, we can get a pretty good idea of what messages his movement subscribed to by reading the Book of James.

James was Jesus's brother and assumed leadership of the messianic movement after Jesus was executed. In the Book of James, James addressed: devotion and obedience to God, fairness to others, caution in speech, the risks of wealth, and the virtues of patience and prayer.

James's messages were rather plain and ordinary compared to Paul's, but they reflected first-century messianic Jewish traditions (and very likely Jesus's own beliefs), far better than Paul's.

The alleged events described in the New Testament regarding Jesus's conception, birth, life, death, and resurrection are irrational. Consequently, there is no reason to accept that the New Testament is divine or even divinely inspired. This means that Christian dogmas are not inviolate and that they can also be transcended without fear.

Islam

The Muslim scripture is the Quran. It is composed of:

- Thirty parts, with
- One hundred and fourteen chapters.

Islam became a formal religion in the seventh century CE with the teachings of Muhammad. However, Muslims maintain that Islam is not a new religion—it is a revival of the ancient religion practiced by Adam, Abraham, Moses, Jesus, and other biblical prophets. Muslims believe that God commanded Muhammad to *reestablish* his *true* laws—laws that had been corrupted through time by Jews and Christians.

Muhammad

The Quran is essentially a compilation of revelations allegedly received by Muhammad—from God—through the angel Gabriel, over a twenty-three-year period of time.

Muslims claim that every copy of the Quran is exactly the same. That may be essentially true for copies printed in Arabic, but English translations vary too much to be evaluated reliably. Consequently, since the Quran was conceived exclusively by Muhammad, evaluating his life seems to be the best way to evaluate the credibility of the Quran.

Muhammad was born in Mecca (Saudi Arabia) in 570 CE.[12] He was orphaned when he was six years old and then raised by his uncle, Abu Talib.

By all accounts, Muhammad's early life was unremarkable. He tended flocks of sheep and goats for the Meccans, and may have occasionally accompanied his uncle on journeys to southern Arabia and Syria.

In 595, he married a rich widow more than twice his age, named Khadija. This marriage provided him with the affluence to spend much of his time alone and in contemplation in the mountains near Mecca.

Muhammad allegedly received his first vision from God in 610 while meditating in a cave on Mount Hira. He claimed that the angel Gabriel appeared to him and commanded him—in the name of God—to promote the "true" religion that would be revealed to him.

He began to preach this religion to the Meccans in 614. Initially, his sermons were tolerated, but by 622 he had alienated them and was driven away—at which time, he traveled to Medina with a group of followers.

There, Muhammad allegedly continued to receive revelations from God, and he became a powerful leader. This transition is recognized as paramount in Islam and marks the beginning of the Islamic calendar (Islamic year 1 corresponds to 622 CE in the Christian Gregorian calendar).

---

12   There are no Muslim dates prior to 622 CE.

In 624, Muhammad solicited, and allegedly received, permission from God to wage war against the "enemies of Islam" (22:39-40). At that time, he led a small force of Muslims who defeated a much larger force of Meccans at Badr.

This victory emboldened Muhammad, and he promptly evicted the Qaynuqa Jews from Medina (confiscating their property), ordered the death of Abu Afak (a Jewish poet who spoke out against him), ordered the death of Asma bint Marwan (a Jewish woman who spoke out against him), ordered the death of Ka'b ibn al-Ashraf (a Jewish poet who spoke out against him), and also evicted the Banu Nadir Jews from Medina.

Beginning in 627 and extending over the next few years, Muhammad massacred the Qurayza Jews at Medina, subjugated the Khabar Jews, and sent emissaries with written demands to foreign leaders to acknowledge him as a *divine* prophet and to accept Islam as their faith.

Muhammad's messengers met with varying degrees of success, but the Christian leader Amru the Ghassanide held so much contempt for Muhammad's demands that he executed the emissary.

In offended response, Muhammad sent three thousand troops against Amru in 629, but Amru—with help from the Greeks—was able to repel the Muslim advance.

That was the first of many conflicts that would occur between Christians and Muslims. Muhammad's defeat encouraged the Meccans to break faith with him, and in defiance they committed several acts of violence against his allies.

In reaction to this defiance, in 630 Muhammad invaded and captured Mecca with ten thousand soldiers. At that time, the Meccans agreed to acknowledge Muhammad as their leader and prophet, which established Islam as the dominant religion in Arabia.

One year later, Muhammad died.

Muslims maintain that Muhammad proffered peace, but history reveals that his life was very violent. Additionally, it appears that the initial acceptance of Islam was accomplished under severe duress.

Recording of the Quran

According to orthodox Muslims, God's revelations were memorized by Muhammad and then recited to his followers—who also memorized and recorded portions of them. This unstructured approach at preserving the Quran was initially considered acceptable. However, after the Battle of Yamama in 633 CE, so many Muslims, who had memorized portions of the Quran, were killed that Abu Bakr, the first Muslim caliph, ordered it to be compiled into a single body of written text. That project was reportedly accomplished within six months of Muhammad's death, but it was not organized into its present form at that time.

Uthman ibn Affan, the third caliph, recognized the need for standardization of the Quran, so he organized a committee who produced the version known as the Uthmanic Codex. It was completed sometime between 650 and 656 CE. At that time standardized copies of it were sent to all of the Muslim provinces, where scribes made more copies of them. It was also at that time that Uthman ordered all previous copies of the Quran, in whole or in part, destroyed.

Muslims claim the current version of the Quran is identical to the original Uthmanic Codex, and that it contains, quite literally, the actual words of God spoken to Muhammad through the angel Gabriel, but that claim cannot be true.

Several existing Quran manuscripts, specifically the Samarqand and Topkapi copies, are believed by many Muslims to be original Uthman texts, but many scholars challenge that claim because they were written in a type of script that was not generally used before the late 700s CE.

Additionally, in 1972, during renovation of the Great Mosque of Sana'a in Yemen, tens of thousands of fragments of text from some of the earliest known copies of the Quran were recovered—some of which exhibited discrepancies from today's Quranic texts.

The earliest extant versions of the Quran date from the late 700s CE. Consequently, Muslims are not in possession of their original scripture or an undisputed, accurate facsimile of it.

Despite what Muslims claim, Islam is not the revival of the ancient religion practiced by Adam, Abraham, Moses, Jesus, and other biblical prophets. It clearly incorporates aspects of Judaism into it, but it also incorporates Christian concepts introduced by Paul in the first century CE.

Islam is a compilation of Judaism and Christianity—from an Arab perspective. As such, it is reasonable to assume that the Quran was not provided to Muhammad by God through the angel Gabriel. Consequently, there is no reason to believe that the Quran is divine, which means that Muslim dogmas are not inviolate and that they can also be transcended without fear.

Abrahamic Religious Contention

The histories of Judaism, Christianity, and Islam are filled with contention and violence. Adherents of these religions have been killing each other continuously to maintain or expand their influences since their inceptions. This is truly puzzling because Jews, Christians, and Muslims all pray to, and believe they receive guidance from, the same God. They also recognize most of the same prophets and angels.[13] So, why does so much animosity exist between them? In order to answer that question, we have to go back and look at the Torah, the Holy Bible, and the Quran from slightly different perspectives.

No one actually knows who wrote the Torah or when it was written. Scholars, however, are fairly certain that it was written by a number of different authors, over an extended period of time. Regardless of who wrote it, or when it was written, it contains extremely polarizing pro-Israelite and

---

13 Jews and Christians do not recognize Muhammad as a prophet.

anti-Egyptian/Arab sentiments. The most polarizing of which is that God favored the Israelites over all other people:

> For thou art a holy people unto HaShem thy God, and HaShem hath chosen thee to be His own treasure out of all peoples that are upon the face of the earth. (Deuteronomy 14:2, etc.)

The second was that God regarded Gentiles (specifically Egyptians and Arabs) with contempt. Anti-Egyptian/Arab sentiments occur throughout the Tanakh, most notably: Abraham's rejection of his half Egyptian son, Ishmael (Genesis 21:9-16); God wreaking havoc on the Egyptians with plagues (Genesis 7-12); and even God helping the Israelites to "smite" various Arab tribes in their conquest of Canaan (Exodus 32:27-29, etc.).

These assertions understandably offended Arabs and Gentiles and severely alienated them.

By the first century CE, some Europeans in the region were ready to adopt monotheism, but because Gentiles had been regarded as inferior to the Israelites in the Torah, there was no temptation to adopt Judaism. However, when Paul introduced Christianity, a new religion that recognized the Jewish god Yahweh—a religion that regarded everyone as equals and offered an afterlife in heaven and did not require great personal sacrifice—it caught on very quickly.

Christians incorporated the Jewish Tanakh into their Bible to enhance Jesus's credibility, but then immediately nullified the Laws of Moses through antinomianism. In so doing, they offended Jews and severely alienated them.[14]

Additionally, by including the Tanakh in their Bible, Christians tacitly supported the Jewish claim that Egyptians and Arabs were inferior to Jews in the eyes of God—inadvertently offending and severely alienating them.

---

14   Some solidarity now exists between Jews and Christians—but only because they share an adversary perceived as more threatening to them, Islam.

By the seventh century CE, Muhammad (an Arab) was willing to adopt monotheism, but because Egyptians and Arabs had been demeaned by Jews and Christians, he established a new religion specifically for Arabs—Islam.

When Muhammad conceived Islam, he decided to recognize the Jewish god, Yahweh, as the *one true god* (as Allah). He also incorporated all of the Jewish prophets and angels from the Tanakh into Islam. However, he claimed that the Tanakh was a corruption of God's laws and that God had provided *him* with the "true" laws so that *he* could reinstate them. This claim naturally offended Jews and permanently alienated them.

Muhammad also acknowledged the existence of Jesus, but regarded him as a prophet—not the son of God. In so doing, he offended Christians and permanently alienated them.

About the only issue that Jews, Christians, and Muslims seem able to agree upon is that only one of them can be right—which means the others must be wrong. Each, of course, passionately believes that its religion is the one true religion as established by God. They also passionately believe that all other religions are false religions created by the devil to lure wayward souls away from the one true religion—and that those who follow those religions are enemies of God and are, therefore, their enemies.

It is one of the great ironies of the Abrahamic religions that adherents of these religions all worship the same god, Yahweh, but they are perpetually at war with each other. As incredulous as it may seem, George W. Bush and Osama bin Laden prayed to—and assumedly believed they were receiving guidance from—the same god, at the same time.

When Abrahamic scriptures are evaluated objectively, it becomes clear that they are indefensibly irrational. Therefore, it is reasonable to assume that they are not accurate facsimiles of texts provided to them by God, and that they are not divine. Consequently, there is no reason to preserve, defend, or advance Jewish, Christian, or Muslim SIGs or their dogmas.

Religious Indoctrination

Religious SIGs receive enormous public support in most cultures. In order for them to receive that support, they must somehow convince people that they provide indispensable services. They generally accomplish that by offering rewards for obedience and by threatening punishments for disobedience.

In the case of Christianity and Islam—the two most successfully promoted religions—reward is the promise of everlasting salvation in heaven for the souls of the obedient, and punishment is the threat of everlasting damnation in hell for the souls of the disobedient.

Christian and Muslim SIGs have never offered any evidence that obedient souls go to heaven, or that disobedient souls go to hell. In fact, they have offered no evidence that souls, heaven, or hell even exist. Nevertheless, Christian and Muslim SIGs have managed to convince more than half the world's population that they do exist—and that the only way to ensure that their souls will go to heaven, rather than hell, is if individuals support them and their dogmas.

Religious SIGs achieve this degree of obedience by initiating their indoctrination campaigns on impressionable young children. Once they have been successfully indoctrinated, continued obedience and support is maintained through a combination of fear of damnation and fear of social condemnation.

Victims of religious indoctrination are effectively, permanently deluded and experience debilitating, psychological consequences; and yet, astoundingly, parents continue to subject their children to religious indoctrination, paradoxically because they have been indoctrinated to believe that it is the only way to ensure that their children's souls will go to heaven when they die.

Blind faith in religious SIGs and their dogmas is very similar to the phenomenon known as Stockholm syndrome. They are equally perverse, but blind faith in religious SIGs and their dogmas is not recognized as such, ironically because it is so widespread that it is considered normal and good. Blind faith in religious SIG's and their dogmas is normalized, and therefore an unrecognized, form of Stockholm syndrome.

Breaking this destructive cycle will be extremely difficult because religious SIGs will argue that it is their right—their duty, even—to indoctrinate children with religious dogmas. Consequently, it is crucial that publics be made aware of the fact that religious dogmas are not divine and that maintaining faith in them, or in the religious SIGs that promote them, impedes the raising of awareness and the adoption of progressive social behavior.

8: Political SIGs

The same processes used to evaluate and transcend religious SIGs can be applied to political SIGs. However, some political SIGs can be selectively embraced while others will need to be transcended.

Operating within most nations are political SIGs, ranging in perspective from liberal to conservative. Each SIG competes against the others for control of governments.

Like religious SIGs, political SIGs also solicit public support. However, *some* liberal political SIGs endeavor to do so through education, while *all* conservative SIGs endeavor to do so through indoctrination.

Consequently, while all conservative political SIGs need to be transcended, liberal political SIGs that encourage progressive social behavior, with some caveats, need to be embraced and supported.

Unfortunately, many liberal political SIGs now maintain unrealistic perspectives, and advocate impractical social behavior because they have had to operate in opposition to the highly irrational perspectives and behavior advocated by opposing conservative political SIGs.

There is no question that liberal political SIGs will have to realign themselves as conservative political SIGs are transcended, but this should not be too difficult for them because they are progressive.

9: Economic SIGs

The third category of SIGs that needs to be addressed is economic SIGs, because faith in them and their dogmas also inhibits the raising of awareness and the adoption of progressive social behavior.

In most countries—including the United States—ideological socialistic and capitalistic economic SIGs vie for dominance within their governments. Each strives to indoctrinate publics to have faith in them and their dogmas, and each believes that its perspectives are worth fighting to maintain or advance.

Socialism is an economic strategy motivated by social equality—based on cooperation—and fueled by resources held in public trust. Socialism is strongly associated with political progressivism and is nondenominational.

Consequently, socialism is—or at least has the potential for being—a sustainable economic strategy. However, because it is based on cooperation rather than competition, it is far less dynamic than, and cannot compete with, capitalism over the short term.

Capitalism is an economic strategy in which commerce is motivated by profit—driven by competition—and fueled by resources held in private ownership. Capitalism is strongly associated with political conservatism, and in the United States, fundamentalist Christianity.

Capitalism is by far the more dynamic and productive strategy, but because it is driven by competition it inevitably leads to profound disparities in the social hierarchy, overexploitation of resources, and severe environmental degradation. Consequently, capitalism is not sustainable and cannot compete with socialism over the long term.

In point of fact, neither economic strategy can be counted on *exclusively* to meet society's short- and long-term needs. Whether societies choose to modify socialism to make it more competitive, or capitalism to make it more sustainable, doesn't really matter. If the strategies employed are realistic and socially and environmentally responsible, they will inevitably end up being very similar.

Whatever economic strategies societies choose to adopt, they need to reward personal achievement. Rewards can vary from social recognition and appreciation to the accumulation of wealth. Ideally, as individuals become more aware, social recognition and appreciation might eventually prove to be more desirable than wealth.

In any event, rational economic strategies must be based on reason—rather than ideologies—so faith in economic SIGs and their dogmas has to be transcended before sustainability can be achieved.

PART III: RAISING AWARENESS

The significant problems we face cannot be solved at the same level of thinking we were at when we created them.

—Albert Einstein

10: Sources of Information

Awareness cannot be raised without having reliable sources of rational information. We receive information throughout our lives from five primary sources: parents, schools, places of worship, the media, and social media. Most of these sources provide some rational information, but none of them can currently be regarded as reliable sources of it.

Parents

It would be nearly impossible to overstate the influence that parents have on their children's awareness—or lack of it—and therefore, on their behavior, throughout their lives. If parents are aware and resist indoctrination, there is a good chance that they will pass on those traits to their children. Conversely, if parents are deluded and susceptible to indoctrination, they likely will pass on those traits to their children.

Unfortunately, most parents today have been thoroughly indoctrinated with dogmas from religious, political, and economic SIGs—which means that they are moderately to severely deluded—which means most parents are not reliable sources of rational information.

This is a tragic situation because parents are naturally inclined to convey information they learned from their parents, to their children. And children are naturally inclined to assimilate information from their parents.

As global awareness increases, parents will be able to resume their natural roles as educators. In the meantime, they will have to rely on schools to provide their children with the rational information they need to adopt progressive social behavior when they mature.

The best that can be hoped for today is that parents will refrain from indoctrinating their children, or allowing others to indoctrinate them.

Schools

Educating today's children is critically important to the future of our species. The only viable way to accomplish this is through *public* education. Consequently, it is essential that public schools remain open, well funded, and staffed with rational teachers, so that they can devote their resources *exclusively* to education, without interference from ideological SIGs and their dogmas.

Publicly funding education may seem like an unfair burden to place on taxpayers, but educating children is requisite to raising global awareness and the only way to ensure that children are adequately educated is through public education. Consequently, whatever the costs, they are worth it. Besides, the costs of *not* publicly funding education are far greater to the public in the long run.

Affluent, conservative members of societies frequently send their children to private schools. Private schools can provide superior education, but most of them are directly or indirectly controlled by religious or political or economic SIGs. Consequently, their curricula include indoctrination campaigns that elicit future student support for themselves and their dogmas.

Graduates of private schools represent a vast minority of graduating students, but their social influences are disproportionately much higher because they are far more likely to become leaders and influential members of religious, political, and economic SIGs.

Consequently, private schools actually inhibit the raising of public awareness and the adoption of progressive social behavior.

It is in all nations' long-term best interests to mandate public education. If all children, even the most privileged, attended public schools, then public schools would be much better funded and staffed. Affluent members of societies would see to that.

No expense should be spared to provide quality education to everyone—everywhere. Education is requisite to raising awareness. Raising awareness is requisite to adopting progressive social behavior. Adopting progressive social behavior is requisite to establishing sustainability.

Places of Worship

Places of worship also profoundly influence public awareness and social behavior, but the information they convey is controlled completely by religious SIGs and is comprehensively irrational. Consequently, places of worship are not—and never will be—reliable sources of rational information.

The Media

According to a Pew Research poll, 57 percent of US adults currently rely on various media outlets to provide them with "news." Unfortunately, most people do not seek out media outlets that convey pertinent rational information. Instead, they seek out, and therefore support, media outlets that convey irrational information that conforms to the dogmas that they have been indoctrinated with throughout their lives.

Because of exposure to relentless indoctrination campaigns by ideological SIGs, most adults are now moderately to severely deluded. Unfortunately, media outlets not only cater to these delusions, they intentionally seek to reinforce them through indoctrination campaigns of their own.

This condition is pervasive throughout the media industry, but it is especially evident with Fox News. It debuted in 1996 when News Corporation founder, chairman, and chief executive officer Rupert Murdoch launched it as a cable news network.

Fox News claims to be "fair and balanced," but its commentary reflects Murdoch's ultra-conservative beliefs, and it strives to indoctrinate the public with irrational information that supports his conservative beliefs.

This leads to an important question: just how much influence can one individual like Rupert Murdoch have on raising or impeding public awareness?

As of 2005, News Corporation owned one hundred cable channels, forty television stations, nine satellite networks, 175 newspapers, forty book publishing imprints, and one movie studio—including Fox News Channel, Fox Business Network, the *New York Post*, the *Wall Street Journal*, *Barron's*, and HarperCollins Publishers.[15] Consequently, in 2005, News Corporation's various media organizations reached an estimated 4.7 billion people worldwide.[16]

This means that individuals like Murdoch have the capacity to profoundly raise public awareness through education—*or* profoundly delude the public through indoctrination. Unfortunately, Murdoch's ultra-conservative beliefs prevail throughout his organizations so he is effectively deluding millions of people—worldwide—every day.

As destructive as this type behavior is, ironically, we have no choice but to allow it to continue because maintaining freedom of speech is requisite to raising awareness, adopting progressive social behavior, and establishing sustainability.

Chronic media indoctrination can only be curbed if publics are free to choose to support media outlets that seek to indoctrinate them—but choose not to.

---

15   http://www.cjr.org/resources/?c=newscorp
16   Kitty and Greenwald 2005, 49

One way or the other media outlets will play a prominent role in determining the fate of civilization. If they endeavor to raise public awareness, we may be able to achieve sustainability—but if they continue to delude us, civilization will inevitably collapse.

It is critically important at this time that we choose to support only media outlets that are committed to raising public awareness.

Social Media

Approximately 38 percent of American adults now rely on Internet sources, including social media outlets such as Instagram, Facebook, LinkedIn, and Twitter, to provide them with pertinent information.[17]

These venues have the advantage of being spontaneous, but there are tremendous risks associated with them because individuals can convey harmful, irrational information to large audiences with complete impunity.

Also, the same problem occurs with social media sites that occurs with mainstream media outlets. People seek social media sites that convey information that supports the dogmas they have been indoctrinated with—and there are many more highly irrational social media sites than mainstream media outlets.

So, once again, we are faced with the problem of how to keep irrational information from being conveyed to the public, without infringing upon freedom of speech. And the solution, once again, is to discourage its acceptance.

This will require that publics raise the bar when assessing the reliability of information they encounter through social media. Fortunately, most noteworthy information is recognized by mainstream media outlets where its credibility is objectively evaluated and commented upon.

---

17   http://www.journalism.org/2016/07/07/pathways-to-news/

In any event, social media sites cannot currently be regarded as reliable sources of pertinent rational information—no matter who is posting that information.

PART IV: EMBRACING REASON

Knowledge will forever govern ignorance; and a people who mean to be their own governors must arm themselves with the power which knowledge gives.

—James Madison

11: Religion

Religions provide no tangible products or services in exchange for lifetimes of servitude and support—and they are directly responsible for most of the polarity and conflict that exists in the world today. Open societies must always defend everyone's right to belief as they choose, but it is their responsibility to raise public awareness to the level where publics choose *not* to believe religious dogmas, or to support religious SIGs.

Sustainability can only be achieved if we embrace reason, and there is *no* reason to support religion.

12: Government

Unlike religions that can be completely transcended, governments are absolutely necessary. However, they must be restructured so that they can progress as our material cultures progress.

A primary obligation of publics is to establish governments that manage their nations sustainably. Pertinently, *no* public has ever yet managed to do this—primarily because they have always allowed religious, political, or business SIGs to gain control of their governments.

In order for governments to manage nations sustainably, they must be free to behave *rationally*, which means that they must never allow ideological SIGs to gain control or unduly influence them.

Religious Influences

Religious influences in governments range from atheistic to theocratic.

Some will argue that atheistic governments are free from irrational beliefs, but that is not the case. The term *atheism* is currently being used casually to denote *a lack of belief in gods*. However, the traditional and more proper definition denotes *the belief that gods do not exist*.

This dual usage is confusing because the former definition denotes a *rational perspective*, whereas the second denotes an *irrational belief*.

Atheistic governments, such as the North Korean government, maintain that gods do not exist, so they are not free from irrational beliefs and cannot govern rationally.

On the other end of the spectrum are theocratic governments, such as the Iranian government. They are based on specific ideological beliefs, so they cannot govern rationally, either.

That leaves secular governments. The United States claims to be a secular government that maintains a strict constitutional separation between church and state, but that claim is nonsense. The only places in the US Constitution that address religion are in Article VI, which states:

- No religious Test shall ever be required as a Qualification to any Office or public Trust under the United States.

And in the First Amendment, which states:

- Congress shall make no law respecting an establishment of religion…

The First Amendment protects the privacy of individuals' beliefs (or lack of beliefs), and is generally interpreted as meaning that Congress cannot mandate a *specific* state religion. However, Christian organizations have gradually gained control over the US government to the degree that it is nearly impossible for someone who does not profess to believe in the Abrahamic God, Yahweh, to be elected or even appointed to a prominent position within the government.

Consequently, contrary to popular belief, the US government is actually a de facto theocracy—which means that it cannot govern rationally, either.

Paradoxically, the only way to establish rational, secular governments is for governments to allow everyone to believe what they choose—and for everyone to choose *not* to believe in religions.

In order for governments to manage nations sustainably, they must behave *rationally*, which means that religious SIGs must never be allowed to control or unduly influence them.

Political Influences

Nations are managed by governments, and governments are managed by political SIGs, or parties, that maintain ideologies ranging from ultra-liberal to ultra-conservative.

Like religious SIGs, political SIGs elicit public support through indoctrination campaigns and firmly believe that their ideologies are *right* and that all others are *wrong*.

Party politics is often lauded as the most effective way to achieve balance in government, but that claim is absurd. The dynamics of party politics virtually assures the perpetuation of severely polarized factions *within* governments—competing with each other for control *of* governments.

The result of this is that *either* liberal *or* conservative perspectives prevail, which means that large numbers of people are chronically underrepresented. This inevitably leads to internal polarity and the pervasive erosion of public trust in governments—a condition that almost everyone should be able to relate to today.

Because we have been indoctrinated to believe in and support various political SIGs and their dogmas, we have failed to recognize that the most important consideration when establishing governments is that they be rational—which means, paradoxically, that we must never allow political SIGs to control or unduly influence them.

Ironically, George Washington realized this and even agreed to serve a second term—against his wishes—in the hope of unifying the nation and transcending the discord that had arisen between political SIGs during his first term as president. Unfortunately, he failed.

Global sustainability can only be achieved if nations establish rational governments, and rational governments can only be established in the absence of political ideologies.

Economic Influences

Economic SIGs, ranging from ideologically socialistic to capitalistic, also seek to gain public support through indoctrination so that they can control or influence governments.

Socialism is based on interdependency, cooperation, and consideration. It also encourages progressive perspectives and social behavior, so socialistic governments have the capacity to manage nations sustainably—over the long term. However, nations managed by socialistic governments cannot survive in competition with capitalistic nations—over the short term.

Conversely, capitalism is based on independency, competition, and exploitation. It encourages conservative perspectives and behavior. Capitalistic governments excel at encouraging growth—over the short term. However, nations managed by capitalistic governments inevitably exhaust their resources, so they cannot survive—over the long term.

Achieving and maintaining national sustainability will require that governments incorporate enough socialistic aspects into them so that they can establish long-term sustainability—and enough capitalistic aspects into them to remain competitive.

In other words, they will have to maintain *rational* economic perspectives, which means that individual economic SIGs must never be allowed to control or unduly influence governments.

Establishing Rational Government

For thousands of years nations have experimented with different forms of governments, hoping to find ones that proved sustainable. So far, none has succeeded.

Our failures stem primarily from our reliance on religious, political, and economic SIGs to control our governments.

This reliance has categorically eliminated any possibility of our establishing rational governments—which has been a tragic mistake because *only* rational governments can be sustainable.

Consequently, all nations should now devote their energies into establishing rational governments. Those that succeed, regardless of where they began, or how they get there, will end up with governments that are remarkably similar—because rational is universal.

13: Commerce

Commerce is integral to civilized existence, and most nations encourage it because the products and services that businesses provide raise standards of living. However, irresponsible commerce profoundly negatively impacts our species, other species, and the environment.

Business SIGs insist that they must be free to operate without governmental regulations in order to provide the products and services that nations need. However, it is essential to realize that business SIGs are devoted to generating profits—not raising living standards—and that their myopic devotion to generating profits entices them to ignore the negative impact their activities have on our species, other species, and the environment.

Free market economies are dynamic and promote growth, which is generally regarded as good for nations, at least over the short-term. However, they contribute to overpopulation, chronic pollution, resource depletion, and species extinctions, which are definitely bad for nations (and the planet) over the long-term.

When liberal administrations are in power, they generally enact protectionist regulations—unfortunately, these regulations inevitably inhibit economic growth and perceived "prosperity."

Conversely, when conservative administrations are in power, they generally decrease regulations—sometimes with positive short-term effects. However, in the end, deregulation almost always leads to financial collapse with profound collateral damage.

Within our irrational ideological flip-flopping political system, this is the best we can do—but it is not good enough.

It is essential that we establish progressive economic strategies that encourage innovation *and* conservation. This will require that we first establish stable rational governments that will closely monitor and regulate commerce—all of which is dependent upon raising public awareness.

PART V: ACHIEVING SUSTAINABILITY

We stand now where two roads diverge. . . The road we have long been traveling is deceptively easy, a smooth superhighway on which we progress with great speed, but at its end lies disaster. The other fork of the road—the one less traveled by—offers our last, our only chance to reach a destination that assures the preservation of the earth.

—Rachel Carson

14: Reprieval

No one knows exactly how many people Earth can support, but that number will correlate closely to how much of Earth's productive land we can claim for our exclusive use without chronically harming Earth's biota.

Currently, we are claiming about 10 percent of Earth's land, but that 10 percent maintains 20 to 40 percent of Earth's potential for biological production.[18]

One species cannot claim that much of Earth's potential without incurring catastrophic consequences. The fact that environmental collapse has not occurred yet should be regarded as an undeserved opportunity to reverse this trend and establish sustainability before it is too late.

---

18   http://www.curiousmeerkat.co.uk/questions/much-land-earth-inhabited/

15: Population

Currently, there are about 7.5 billion people on Earth—which is arguably at least twice as many as Earth can sustain—and yet we continue to allow our population to grow.

The United Nations is currently predicting that our population will increase to just over 10 billion by 2100,[19] but that prediction is just math. When considering resource depletion, pollution, environmental degradation, and other factors, it seems far more likely that our population will crash long before it reaches that level.

The only way to avoid that calamity is to rapidly lower our population.

National survival, at least until quite recently, depended upon growing populations, so proposing population reduction will be met with extreme resistance by almost everyone. This resistance will manifest itself primarily from three conservative positions: state security, perpetuation of religions, and individuals' right to procreate.

State Security

It is not known exactly where, when, or why the first war was fought. But it is a pretty safe bet that it was fought somewhere in the Middle East around ten thousand years ago in competition for land—and that the aggressors claimed that their actions were sanctified by their gods.

We are now fighting wars with far more sophisticated weapons, but we are fighting them for exactly the same reasons. As long as nations rely on competition for resources—and maintain faith in ideological SIGs and their dogmas to guide their behaviors—they will continue to fight wars.

And as long as nations fight wars, they will need to grow perpetually larger and stronger so that they can compete with, and defend themselves from, other competitive nations that are growing perpetually larger and stronger,

19 http://news.sciencemag.org/scienceinsider/2011/05/10-billion-plus-why-world-population.html

so that they can compete with and defend themselves from other competitive nations, and on and on.

International trade has progressed to the point where nations no longer have to fight wars over resources. However, inertia compels many nations to continue to build and maintain large armies even though, for most of them, overpopulation now threatens their future prospects far more than not having a large army to defend them does.

A better strategy for ensuring state security would be to establish an international agency empowered to defend *all* national borders. It is unlikely that any nation would invade another nation if they knew that international sanctions would be instantly imposed upon them, and that international forces would promptly be deployed to oppose them.

The potential benefits of having some form of an *International Guard* are enormous. Nations would no longer need to develop, or maintain, weapons of mass destruction, nor would they have to build up and maintain large armies to defend themselves. If all nations felt secure from invasion, they could restore their populations to environmentally sustainable levels.

Perpetuation of Religions

Religions also contribute to rampant population growth. Their existences depend upon continuing support from members, and the most expedient way to increase membership is by encouraging existing members to have more children, which they do by discouraging or forbidding members from practicing birth control.

It is unlikely that religions could survive today if they did not have access to young children to indoctrinate. Their beliefs are simply too improbable to solicit much support from objective adults. Consequently, in the interest of their own self-preservation, most religions will adamantly resist population reduction, at least among their own members.

There is no way to break this destructive cycle other than by transcending faith in religious SIGs and their dogmas.

"Right" to Procreate

Many people insist that it is their right—or even God's intention—to allow conceptions to occur naturally. That would be a reasonable argument if they lived in a natural state of existence, but they do not. They live in an artificial state of existence.

In natural states of existence, natural selection would prevail. Conceptions would occur almost every time women came into estrus, but many women or their babies would die due to pregnancy complications. Those who argue that it is their right to procreate naturally would then logically also have to accept the consequences of dying naturally.

In modern nations, we all benefit from artificial technologies that save or prolong our lives, but those benefits have costs and responsibilities; one of which is managing our population responsibly.

Population Reduction

We have been completely remiss in managing our population. And as difficult as it may be to manage, it will be even more difficult to reduce it. Nevertheless, that is exactly what we have to do now, and the most humane and equitable way to accomplish this is by reducing birthrates.

Remarkably, we have no idea how many people Earth can sustain, but we do know that our current population of 7.5 billion is way too high.

With objective research in the future, we will be able to determine more accurately what sustainable population levels should be. In the meantime, it would be prudent to begin by reducing our population by 50 percent over the next fifty to sixty years. This is roughly equivalent to the population increase that occurred over the previous fifty to sixty years.

If each couple produces (on average) one child for the next sixty years, the world population will drop to 3,140,625,000 by 2070. This decrease seems like a lot, but it is actually less than the increase that occurred over the previous sixty years. For comparative purposes, if each couple averages two children, the population will remain the same, and obviously, if each couple averages more than two children, the population will continue to increase. Once our population is reduced to a sustainable level, a procreation ratio of 1:1 (two children per couple) will maintain it.

This may seem like an impossible goal to achieve, but if the public is made aware of the risks associated with overpopulation, are freed from pressures imposed upon them by societies and religions to have large families, and are provided with safe contraceptives, many couples would voluntarily choose to have fewer children.

The key to reducing our population is raising global awareness, so no expense should be spared by progressive nations to raise awareness in third-world countries. Global funding for education would arguably be the wisest use of capital allocated for foreign aid—by a substantial margin.

For couples who insist on having more than one child—let them. Governments have offered tax incentives to couples to have more children for thousands of years. They can now offer increasingly favorable tax incentives to couples who have fewer than two children—and increasingly severe disincentives to couples who have more than one child.

(Obviously, increased taxes should not be imposed on couples who already have more than one child or to couples in the future who experience multiple births per pregnancy.)

This approach is fair because couples who have more children place greater demands on their governments to provide for them.

It is important to realize that our population will be reduced. We can reduce it artificially to sustainable levels—in which case, civilization will continue—or we can wait for it to occur naturally—in which case, our population will crash, along with civilization.

Ultimately, reducing our population to sustainable levels will require that we transcend faith in religious, political, and economic SIGs and their dogmas—and embrace reason. Only then can we fully realize that we are all members of a single species, that we are all interrelated, that we are all interdependent, and that we all need to cooperate with each other for our common good.

16: Pollution

Another negative effect of conservative social behavior is the proliferation of chemical and organic pollutants. In an incredibly short period of time, we have managed to pollute virtually all of Earth's air, water, and land.

There are many pollutants that will have to be dealt with in the future, but none is more pressing than carbon dioxide, so it alone will be addressed here. If we can raise our awareness enough to manage carbon dioxide pollution, we should have no problem dealing with other forms of pollution.

Carbon Dioxide

Carbon dioxide is not normally considered a pollutant. In fact, life could not exist without it. However, by definition, when any chemical occurs in harmful concentrations, it must be regarded as a pollutant, and that is definitely the case with carbon dioxide today.

We emit carbon into the atmosphere through the burning of fossil fuels, clearing forests, making cement, and other activities intrinsic to civilized existence. In the atmosphere, carbon atoms combine with oxygen atoms to form carbon dioxide.

Anthropogenic carbon accounts for less than 4 percent of the total amount released into the atmosphere each year, but that is enough to seriously disrupt the carbon balance.

Ice core studies indicate that since the dawn of the Industrial Revolution, atmospheric carbon dioxide levels have increased from a normal level of about 280 parts per million (ppm) to 400 ppm, and that number is continuing to rise (Figure 1).

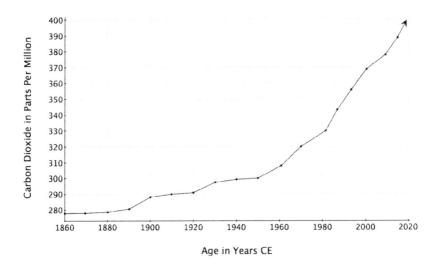

Figure 1: Carbon dioxide increase since the dawn of the Industrial Revolution

Climate Change

Meteorologists believe that anthropogenic carbon dioxide is responsible for the current global warming trend. This is a reasonable assumption since carbon dioxide is an insulating greenhouse gas, humans are introducing about 40 billion tons of it into the atmosphere every year, and global temperatures are rising.

However, Earth's climate is influenced by a myriad of complex celestial and terrestrial events that have to be considered when determining the causes of climate change.

Earth's climate is divided into glacial ages. Each age is composed of cooling episodes known as glacials and warming episodes known as interglacials.

Glacials and interglacials are brought on by three cyclic celestial events: eccentricity of Earth's orbit, axial tilt, and precession of equinoxes—known collectively as the Milankovitch cycles.[20]

Occurring within glacial and interglacial episodes are cooling periods known as stades and warming periods known as interstades. Stades and interstades are caused by celestial events (such as increasing or decreasing sunspot activity), terrestrial events (such as plate tectonics, volcanic eruptions, increasing or decreasing atmospheric insulation), and other presently unknown conditions.

Stades and interstades can profoundly influence Earth's climate, but their effects are generally, *relatively* short term (Figure 2).

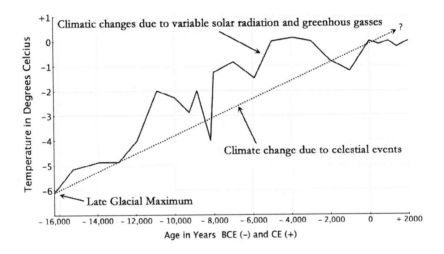

Figure 2: Variations in Earth's temperature since the LGM

The dotted line in Figure 3 shows Earth's temperature increase due to the Milankovitch cycles since the Late Glacial Maximum (LGM) eighteen thousand years ago. The erratic solid line shows the fluctuations in Earth's

---

20   Named for the Serbian mathematician Milutin Milanković, who first calculated their effects on Earth's climate

actual mean temperatures due to stades and interstades over the same time period.[21]

It is essential to recognize that Earth's temperature increased by more than 6°C (10.8°F) between the LGM eighteen thousand years ago and the Industrial Revolution *without any human intervention*—and that it was continuing to rise when the Industrial Revolution began. Consequently, it is impossible to know for certain how much of the current temperature increase is attributable to anthropogenic causes, and how much of it is attributable to natural causes.

From a geological perspective, a 0.7°C (1.26°F) increase is neither abnormal nor particularly alarming. From a human perspective, however, an increase of an additional few degrees could render Earth's most productive ecosystems too hot or arid to support agriculture. It would also be enough to melt the polar ice caps, which would raise ocean levels enough to flood our coastal cities.

These problems are not so much the result of escalating temperature increases, but that temperatures have reached a critical level where any additional increases will profoundly adversely affect us.

Any significant increase in Earth's mean temperature, regardless of the cause, could precipitate the collapse of civilization. Consequently, even if anthropocentric carbon dioxide pollution is only nominally contributing to global warming, we need to curb it. ASAP.

Ocean Acidification

As disturbing as global warming is, when it comes to carbon dioxide pollution, we unfortunately have even bigger and more pressing concerns.

Carbon dioxide pollution is acidifying Earth's oceans at an alarming rate. Oceans absorb about 25 percent of the carbon dioxide introduced into the atmosphere. Scientists have been aware of this condition for a long time

---

21   Determined from ice core studies in Greenland

and have regarded it as a positive moderating influence to the harmful effects of *atmospheric* carbon dioxide pollution. However, when carbon dioxide dissolves in seawater, the water becomes acidic.[22]

Oceanographers have noted that the rate of ocean acidification since the beginning of the Industrial Revolution has increased dramatically. Certainly nothing comparable to it has occurred in the last 21 million years. And although the pH of Earth's oceans is not yet severely, adversely affecting marine biota, the projected increase in acidification is expected to do just that (Figure 3).

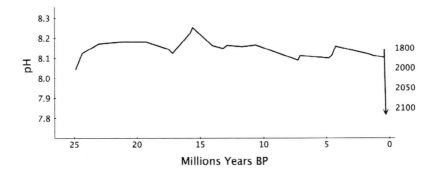

Figure 3: Ocean acidification over the last 21 million years

Oceanographers are predicting that if the increase continues at its present rate, there will be severe oceanic biota loss by 2050 and near total collapse of biota in many areas of the oceans by 2100.

Most of the life-forms that would be directly, adversely affected by acidification are minute organisms, whose diminishment may not seem that important, but they form the base of the food chain for the entire marine ecosystem.[23] Their loss or diminishment—besides being catastrophic to marine biota—would also be catastrophic to terrestrial biota because these minute organisms are responsible for nearly half of the photosynthetic

---

22 Unless otherwise noted, the following information in this section was obtained from the Ocean Acidification Network website (http://www.ocean-acidification.net/FAQacidity. html).

23 http://www.global-greenhouse-warming.com/ocean-acidification.html

activity on Earth.[24] In other words, they produce more oxygen than all of Earth's trees combined—so their loss would lead to increasing levels of atmospheric carbon dioxide—which would lead to further global warming and increased ocean acidification—exacerbating the problem.

Presently, most scientists believe that if we keep atmospheric carbon dioxide levels below 550 ppm (expected by 2050) we would avoid severe climate change problems. However, oceanographers are now warning that carbon dioxide concentrations over 450 ppm would begin to eliminate the saturation zones hospitable to marine life from higher- and lower-latitude oceans. Consequently, they are recommending an absolute atmospheric carbon dioxide concentration ceiling of 450 ppm. Alarmingly, at the present rate of increase, that level will be reached by 2030.

Curbing the release of carbon into the atmosphere has to be done, and it has to be done very soon. But how can we accomplish this?

Curbing Carbon Dioxide Pollution

In order to reduce carbon dioxide pollution, we will have to significantly reduce the amount of carbon we release into the atmosphere. Dramatically reducing our population is the logical first step in this endeavor, but we will also need to reduce the amount of fossil fuels we burn, alter our forestry practices, and alter our diets.

Electrical Generation

Approximately 41 percent of anthropogenic carbon emissions come from burning coal to generate electricity.[25] In recent years, electrical generation stations in the United States have switched from coal to natural gas—a decision that has significantly lowered our carbon footprint.

---

24 hhttp://www.mbari.org/staff/conn/botany/phytoplankton/phytoplankton_coccolithophorids.htm

25 https://www.co2.earth/global-co2-emissions

The United States would like everyone to think that environmental concerns prompted this decision, but that is not true.

The reason that generating stations switched from coal to gas is that recently developed technologies in horizontal drilling and fracking have produced an abundance of natural gas, so it is now more cost effective to burn gas than coal. Their decision to switch was driven by profits.

The fact that the United States has lowered carbon emissions is a good thing, but even if all electrical generation stations switched to natural gas worldwide (which is impossible), that would not solve our problem. We need to stop burning fossil fuels to generate electricity.

Alternative Energy Sources

Many environmentalists believe that all of our energy needs can be supplied by renewables such as: solar, wind, tides, waves, geothermal, and so on. Continued research and development should continue in all of these fields. However, to think that they will ever be able to supply all of our energy needs is incredibly naïve, and committing our future to them would be suicidal.

So what other options do we have?

Nuclear Energy

Actually, there is only one realistic option—fission. Because of several recent accidents at nuclear power plants, however, the public has developed irrational fears regarding nuclear energy and are now resistant to its further development and use.

There is no getting around the fact that fission is potentially dangerous—but how dangerous is it compared to other forms of electrical generation?

Estimates vary widely, but according to the World Health Organization, approximately 7 million people die prematurely each year due to air pollution—the major contributor to which is coal-fired power plants.[26]

By contrast, since the first reactor was built in Obninsk, Russia, in 1954, there have been fewer than fifty deaths reported from radiation poisoning stemming from civilian nuclear electrical generation. And most of these deaths were plant employees at Chernobyl, a facility that did not follow safety guidelines that are generally adhered to everywhere else in the world.

This means that more people die from burning fossil fuels to generate electricity *every hour* than have died from using fission to generate electricity over the last sixty years!

Of perhaps equal concern to people who are wary of nuclear energy is the risk of later development of cancer from exposure to radiation.

Populations around Chernobyl have been closely monitored since the accident in 1986. Non-fatal thyroid cancer incidents in children definitely increased—and future cancer deaths are anticipated—but predictions regarding them vary enormously. The World Health Organization estimated that there may eventually be a total of four thousand deaths related to the Chernobyl incident, but the actual number could be higher or lower.

Critics cite Chernobyl as an example of the risks associated with nuclear energy. This is understandable, but not realistic. Chernobyl did not incorporate containment safety features into its design that are standard features today.

Another legitimate but aggrandized concern regarding nuclear energy is the disposal of radioactive waste. Disposal does present legitimate concerns, but it can be accomplished safely. Besides, we now have the technology to reprocess spent fuel—on site—over and over again, until it no longer presents significant risks to the public or to the environment.

---

26   http://www.who.int/mediacentre/news/releases/2014/air-pollution/en/

This approach greatly minimizes the need for uranium production and waste disposal.

There are definitely risks associated with using fission to generate electricity. However, it is pertinent to note that even after tsunamis severely damaged the Fukushima Daiichi plant in Japan in 2011, there were no acute injuries or deaths to workers or to the public due to exposure to radiation, according to the World Health Organization.

At this time, it is essential that we overcome our irrational fears regarding the use of fission to generate electricity because fission is the only method that can meet our energy needs that does not emit carbon into the atmosphere.

It is time that we realize that civilization is not individual nations rising above others—it is all nations progressing together. Carbon dioxide pollution and electrical generation are global issues that need to be addressed globally.

With that in mind, we should be encouraging the world's brightest scientists to work together to determine the most efficient way to generate electricity with fission. We should also be encouraging the world's brightest engineers to work together to establish designs for building safe nuclear power plants.

Once designs are proven reliable, they can be standardized and used internationally. Utilizing standardized designs would minimize costs and ensure optimal efficiency and safety.

Whether nuclear power plants are run by governments or corporations for profit, they will have to be strictly regulated by an international organization, such as the International Atomic Energy Agency, an organization established in 1957 specifically to advance the peaceful use of nuclear energy.

Transportation

Currently, 27 percent of carbon emissions come from burning fossil fuels in internal combustion engines used in transportation.

Today we associate transportation with internal combustion engines, while we regard electric cars as novelties. However, even before the Model T was introduced, Henry Ford and Thomas Edison collaborated on building electric cars. Edison was not able to produce practical batteries, so the concept was never realized. However, both individuals thought that cars in the future would be powered by electricity.

We now have the ability to produce long-lasting batteries suitable for automotive—and even heavy truck—use. Consequently, we can now begin to rely on electric cars and trucks. This means we will need to generate even more electricity in the future than has been anticipated. This is another reason why we will have to rely on fission to produce electricity in the future.

Learning to rely on electricity to power transportation is an aspect of adopting progressive social behavior.

Diet

Lowering our population, utilizing fission to produce electricity, and relying on electricity to power our vehicles are requisite to curbing carbon dioxide pollution, but the behavioral change that would make the most profound and immediate impact would be changing our diets.

For the vast majority of our species' history, we were essentially vegans. No one knows for certain exactly why or when we began eating meat, but it is reasonable to assume that changing environmental conditions forced us to.

Our metabolisms are able to process animal products reasonably well, but they evolved over many millions of years to process plants. According to Dr. Williams C. Roberts from the National Institutes of Health at Baylor University:

The appendages of carnivores are claws; those of herbivores are hands or hooves. The teeth of carnivores are sharp; those of herbivores are mainly flat (for grinding). The intestinal tract of carnivores is short (3 times body length); that of herbivores, long (12 times body length). Body cooling of carnivores is done by panting; herbivores, by sweating. Carnivores drink fluids by lapping; herbivores, by sipping. Carnivores produce their own vitamin C, whereas herbivores obtain it from their diet. Thus, humans have characteristics of herbivores, not carnivores.[27]

Additionally, our livers, when processing animal products, produce levels of cholesterol that lead to atherosclerosis—a condition that kills us more frequently than any other cause. It is reasonable to assume that if we had evolved to be omnivores or carnivores, this would not be the case. It is pertinent to note that *no* other species that consumes animal products suffers from this condition—just us.

Nevertheless, for about the last hundred-thousand years, we have had no choice but to incorporate animal products into our diets because suitable vegetable products were not always available. That is no longer the case. A wide variety of fresh, frozen, canned, and dried vegetable products are now available to us year-round.

We continue to rely on animal products, partly as a matter of cultural habit, but also partly because the United States Department of Agriculture (USDA) is dual-tasked with promoting healthy diets *and* promoting the sale of agricultural products, including meat and dairy products.

These responsibilities are completely incompatible. The USDA encourages us to consume animal products that diminish—rather than promote—good health. In fact, we would all be healthier if we refrained from consuming animal products entirely.

Unfortunately, our reliance on protein from animal sources is increasing as our population and affluence increase. Surprisingly, more agricultural

---

27   http://meatyourfuture.com/2015/09/herbivores-carnivores/

land is now devoted to raising crops to feed livestock—than crops to feed people, a trend that is proving devastating for the environment.

Approximately 70 percent of the rain forests being cleared in the Amazon today, for example, are being cleared to create range or cropland for livestock. Tragically, the agricultural productivity of this land is less than ten years. Their topsoil's are typically very shallow and quickly depleted. Once that happens, the land frequently turns into unproductive desert. Consequently, hundreds of thousands of acres of lush rain forest are permanently destroyed each year to produce cheap exportable beef.[28]

Clearing rain forests—to create rangeland—to raise more beef is profoundly stupid. Rain forests provide environments for a wide variety of critical biota, trees convert massive amounts of carbon dioxide into oxygen through photosynthesis, and they store immense amounts of carbon in their trunks and limbs. When rain forests are logged and burned, all of those benefits are lost—in many cases, effectively, forever.

Another concern regarding livestock production is that it is a major source of water pollution. The USDA estimates that 500 million tons of manure are produced annually by livestock and poultry[29]—most of which is stored in large open-air lagoons that are prone to leaks and spills that severely, adversely affect aquatic biota in streams, rivers, lakes, and oceans.

Additionally, livestock production is incredibly inefficient. It takes seventy-eight calories of fossil fuel, for example, to produce one calorie of protein from beef, and 5,214 gallons of water to produce one pound of beef. In the United States, 30 percent of our energy resources are currently devoted exclusively to livestock production.[30]

And lastly, livestock is responsible for approximately 18 percent of the total global greenhouse gas emissions. According to the Livestock, Environment

---

28   http://www.converge.org.nz/pirm/ofow.htm

29   http://www.theenvironmentalblog.org/2008/05/farm-animal-waste-an-environmental-hazard/

30   http://www.converge.org.nz/pirm/ofow.htm

and Development Initiative, livestock contributes 9 percent of the carbon dioxide and 37 percent of the methane emissions worldwide.[31]

The single most significant contribution we can make as individuals to curbing carbon dioxide pollution is to stop supporting livestock production by adopting plant-based diets.

17: Conservation

Terrestrial Flora

Nearly 90 percent of Earth's terrestrial biota exists in forests. Unfortunately, encroachment and irresponsible harvesting practices are profoundly, negatively impacting these forests—and with them Earth's terrestrial biota.

Before human intervention, more than 50 percent of Earth's land surface was forested. We have already cut down 80 percent of old-growth forests, some of which we are allowing to regenerate, but much of the land that was originally forested has been claimed exclusively for agricultural use. Consequently, only about 25 percent of Earth is now forested.[32]

Deforestation is escalating in Asia, Africa, and South America. More than sixty thousand square miles of forests are lost every year, and much of that loss is old-growth rain forests that harbor the greatest amount of biotic diversity. Consequently, their loss disproportionately, adversely affects many other species.

North America and Europe are trending toward reforestation, and although the old-growth forests and the biodiversity they once supported cannot be brought back immediately, very positive, recuperative effects are being noted.

31 http://woods.stanford.edu/cgi-bin/focal.php?name=livestock&focal_area=land_use_and_conservation

32 http://www.globalchange.umich.edu/globalchange2/current/lectures/deforest/deforest.html

Unfortunately, the same degree of recuperation is not occurring in tropical zones. They are apparently capable of *sustaining* healthy forests, but not *regenerating* them once they have been cut down. In fact, the end result of deforestation in tropical zones is—ironically—desertification. When that occurs, the land becomes incapable of supporting anything more than impoverished biota.

Besides the detrimental effects deforestation has on local biota, it also profoundly negatively impacts Earth's atmosphere and oceans. Trees assimilate enormous amounts of carbon dioxide from the atmosphere and store it as carbon in their trunks and limbs. When they are cut down, they no longer absorb carbon. Worse, when they are burned (which is typically the case when claiming land for agricultural use), the carbon is released back into the environment.

Some of this carbon goes into the ground, but much of it combines with oxygen in the atmosphere, producing carbon dioxide. Some of that carbon dioxide acts as a greenhouse gas (contributing to global warming), and some of it is absorbed by Earth's oceans (contributing to ocean acidification).

Additionally, it now appears that deforestation changes local climates. The dynamics behind this phenomenon are not well understood, but many regions that have been deforested now receive less rainfall than they did before their forests were cut down.[33]

It is not known what percentage of Earth's land can be cleared and still remain healthy. However, in order to conserve Earth's remaining biota, and minimize the release of carbon into the environment, it is essential that we refrain from cutting down *any* more old-growth forests—and that we enable much of the areas that have already been logged to regenerate.

The key to accomplishing these goals is in raising *global awareness* through education. In the meantime, as individuals, we can encourage forest conservation by boycotting products that contribute to deforestation—and as

---

33   http://www.magicalliance.org/Forests/deforestation_decreases_rainfall.htm

nations, we can impose sanctions on countries that maintain irresponsible forestry practices.

Terrestrial Fauna

Several megafaunal species in North America went extinct around twelve thousand years ago—just *after* humans arrived there. Consequently, there is a temptation to attribute those extinctions to human predation.

However, many megafaunal extinctions occurred just *before* humans arrived in North America, so it is more likely that rapidly changing post-glacial climates and environments were responsible for those extinctions.

Extinctions since then, however, are clearly proportionally linked to increases in human population—some from encroachment and others from *commercial* overhunting. Commercial hunting began in the mid-1800s, and it very quickly led to a number of species extinctions and near extinctions.

Estimates of faunal extinction rates from human activity vary tremendously, but nearly everyone agrees that Earth is losing faunal species at a faster rate today than at any time in the last 4.5 billion years.[34]

Most terrestrial animal species in *most* areas are now protected from over-hunting—and *most* threatened and endangered species in *most* areas are now fully protected. However, markets have recently developed specifically to provide endangered species to perverse clienteles.

Tremendous efforts are currently expended to preserve select endangered species that are perceived especially desirable—such as panda bears and California condors. While it is important to protect these "poster" species, our primary concern should be to preserve biotic diversity. While we are devoting our energies toward a very few—very select—very visible species,

---

[34] https://www.theguardian.com/environment/2015/jun/19/humans-creating-sixth-great-extinction-of-animal-species-say-scientists

countless others that are less visible, or less attractive, are being destroyed every day.

Poignantly, the only way to know how many terrestrial, animal species can be lost to artificial development before Earth's biodiversity is chronically compromised is to exceed that number, at which time Earth's ecosystems—and civilization—will collapse.

In light of these risks, it would be prudent to assume that we have already reached that number—so we must curb further encroachment and over-harvesting Earth's remaining terrestrial animal species.

Increasing global education and awareness are key to fulfilling these progressive responsibilities.

Marine Fauna

The over-harvesting of marine fauna is actually of greater current concern than the over-harvesting of terrestrial fauna. This problem is exacerbated by the fact that over-harvesting oceans is invisible to us on the surface.

Nevertheless, there is now irrefutable evidence that commercial fishing is drastically reducing the populations of nearly every harvestable species of marine organism.

In 1989, a record 95 million tons of fish were harvested worldwide. Since then, there have been significant declines, especially in the Atlantic, Pacific, and Mediterranean oceans. In 1994, crashes in haddock, cod, and yellow-tail flounder species—once thought to be inexhaustible—prompted officials to close six thousand square miles off the coast of Massachusetts to commercial fishing.[35]

The same conditions prevail nearly everywhere. The populations of all species of harvestable marine organisms are declining—rapidly. According to a 1995 report by the United Nations and the Food and Agriculture

---

35   http://www.converge.org.nz/pirm/frames/fish!f.htm

Organization, the "situation is globally non-sustainable, and major ecological and economic damage is already visible."

Another study conducted by twelve scientists from the United States, Canada, Sweden, and Panama concluded that there may be a "global collapse" of harvestable species by 2050.[36]

The scientists involved in the study admit that their dire predictions are not definitive. However, Boris Worm of Dalhousie University in Nova Scotia, the leader of the investigation, stated in an interview that all of the evidence supports this prediction. According to Worm, they:

> extracted all data on fish and invertebrate catches from 1950 to 2003 within all 64 large marine ecosystems worldwide . . . [which] produced 83 percent of global fisheries yields over the past 50 years.

When Worm analyzed the data from the study and extrapolated it into the future, he found it indicated a "100 percent collapse" by 2048. At first, he did not believe the results, but after rechecking all of the data and calculations, he felt compelled to state:

> I do not have a crystal ball, and I do not know what the future will bring, but this is a clear trend . . . there is an end in sight, and it is within our lifetimes.

In response to this, some national and international restrictions have been placed on specific species, but tragically the reaction of many conservative nations has been to encourage the building of larger and more efficient boats to harvest diminishing populations more aggressively. Nevertheless, researchers think that if comprehensive restrictions are initiated and enforced then many marine species would recover.

Placing restrictions on specific marine species, however, does not solve the problem; it frequently just transfers additional pressure onto other species

---

36   http://www.nytimes.com/2006/11/03/world/americas/03iht-fish.3383558.html

that are not protected, thereby jeopardizing their populations. This is a serious concern, because marine ecosystems are so sensitive that over-harvesting *any* species—from shrimp to sharks—directly and indirectly adversely affects *all* species.

Currently, approximately 16 percent of our protein comes from marine organisms. In the future, that percentage will drop dramatically, either because we voluntarily stop harvesting and consuming marine organisms so that their populations can recover or because we have exhausted them.

If we exhaust them, marine ecosystems will collapse—and if marine ecosystems collapse, so will civilization because marine and terrestrial species are interdependent. The only way to avoid collapse is to commit to conserving marine ecosystems—NOW.

Progressive Behavior

Since our ancestors crossed the threshold between primitive and civilized existences twelve thousand years ago, advancing technologies have enabled our population to increase from a pre-agricultural level of about 2 million to the present level of over 7 billion!

This increase is frequently regarded as evidence of our success—and to a certain degree, it is—but the negative impact that artificial development is having on Earth's terrestrial and marine biota is now threatening, rather than enhancing, our future survival prospects.

It is essential that we commit to conserving *all* of Earth's remaining species. This will require a degree of global awareness that we currently do not have—and are not likely to gain at the present rate of increase—in time to avert disaster.

Consequently, the most aware individuals in nations—and the most aware nations within the global community—will have to enact regulations that mandate responsible conservation policies.

Selfish individuals, corporations, and governments will no doubt resist regulations because encroachment and over-harvesting can be very profitable. However, a rational argument can be made that no individual, corporation, or government has the right to chronically degrade Earth's biota.

This degree of conservation may seem impossible to implement, but it is not. We cannot let it be. For the sake of all future generations, we must do whatever it takes to conserve a healthy planet; it is the only conscionable one available to us.

EPILOGUE

Humans have evolved in spatially separate and diverse climates and terrains over many thousands of years, which accounts for our diverse physical appearances and unique cultural traits. However, it is critical to realize that it is not these overt traits that separate us. It is our unrelenting faith in religious, political, and economic SIGs—and their dogmas that divide us into polarized factions.

Despite our outward differences, we are all still members of the same species.

We all share the same aspirations and fears, and regardless of our backgrounds, we all recognize and adore justice—just as we all recognize and abhor injustice.

Unfortunately, we have all been indoctrinated to regard people with different religious, political, and economic beliefs as enemies. And once people are treated as enemies, they become enemies.

Only by transcending faith in ideological SIGs and by embracing reason will we be able to recognize our commonality, which in turn will enable us to pursue global interdependency and cooperation.

In recognition of these progressive goals, it would be prudent to establish ways to demonstrate global solidarity.

One approach would be to divise a global flag that is flown *above* our national flags. With this simple gesture, we would all be reminded that our primary loyalties must be to our species if we are ever to achieve global sustainability.

Another demonstration of solidarity would be the establishment of international holidays. This would be easy, because perfectly appropriate, celebratable events already exist:

- the spring equinox (March 21),
- the summer solstice (June 21),
- the autumn equinox (September 21)
- the winter solstice (December 21)[37]

The celebration of these events would help everyone recognize four critically important, but easily overlooked, annual, celestial occurrences that affect not only our species but all species.

For many thousands of years, our ancestors *did* recognize and celebrate them—and probably still would if Christian SIGs had not forbidden them. They accomplished this in part by gradually replacing the winter solstice with Christmas and the spring equinox with Easter.

International recognition and celebration of solstices and equinoxes would help to establish a degree of international solidarity that has never existed before. Four times each year, people everywhere on Earth would have the opportunity to celebrate something in common, although in their own unique way.

All people are closely related to each other—and all people are distantly related to all other species. The sooner we realize this, the sooner we will learn to cooperate with each other and achieve sustainability.

All of which is dependent upon embracing reality.

---

37   These dates would apply everywhere on Earth, except that in the southern hemisphere, they would be celebrating opposite seasons.